5
1
0

Acknowledgements

Special thanks to my husband Mike for his love and encouragement.

I would also like to thank Trevor Verral for the photography,

Anne Killick for her help in making this book,

and Jacqui Kelly for encouraging me to keep going.

First published in 2009 by

Frankly Sweet Publications, 47 Yew Tree Road, Tunbridge Wells, Kent, UK. TN4 0BG

www.franklysweet.co.uk

Distributed by Search Press Ltd, Wellwood, North Farm Road, Tunbridge Wells, Kent, UK. TN2 3DR

www.searchpress.com

tel: 0044(0)1892 510850 fax: 0044(0)1892 515903

Design, text and photography copyright © Frances McNaughton 2009

Frances McNaughton has asserted her right under the Copyright, Designs and Patents Act 1988

A catalogue record for this book is available from the British Library

ISBN 978-0-9549761-1-8

modelling
fancy-dress
babies

frances mcnaughton

FS
Frankly Sweet
Publications

contents

foreword

After the success of 'Modelling Fairies in Sugar', Frances has come up with another wonderfully vibrant book which will be immensely popular with her fans and many newcomers to modelling and Sugarcraft.

Since 2005, when her last book was published, Frances has been in demand in Holland, Ireland and the USA and has remained as popular as ever in the UK. She has also been involved in the Advertising and Film Industry. The recent award winning Skoda advertising campaign and the film 'Charlie and the Chocolate Factory' showcased her work.

Versatile and talented, I know that many, many people will enjoy her easy-going style, her humour and of course, the subject matter. Her step-by-step approach to modelling ensures that even the most inexperienced will be able to produce work to a very fine quality.

Fairies inspired by her book, have been seen adorning many cakes and competition entries over the last few years, and I'm certain that very soon her delightful Fancy Dressed Babies will start to appear as well.

Eddie Spence MBE

January 2009

modelling fancy-dress babies

introduction

In writing this book I would like to show you how to make these cuddly babies, combining basic simple modelling and using a mould with detailed painting for the face. I chose to use a mould for the face to make the model look like a real baby, dressed-up. The models can be made using different modelling pastes;

edible

sugarpaste - available from supermarkets and sugarcraft shops.

sugar Modelling Paste - sugarpaste with Tylose®, CMC or Gum Tragacanth added.

sugar Mexican Paste - commercially available from specialist sugarcraft shops, or it can be made at home.

non-edible

artista® - an air-drying modelling paste - see suppliers list.

coronet cold porcelain modelling paste® - an air-drying modelling paste - see suppliers   list.

polymer clay - e.g. fimo® and sculpey® - available from craft and art shops.

There are, of course, many other materials which can be used to make these models. You may already have a preference. I like to work in sugar, so the instructions for each model are for making them in sugar. The method of making the shapes for the babies will be the same, but please refer to the manufacturer's instructions in the case of non-edible pastes.

modelling with sugar

The modelling pastes I have used are sugarpaste for the bodies and Mexican Paste for the face and hands. I prefer to use commercially available pastes, as the texture tends to be consistent. Occasionally the sugarpaste is a bit soft, so small pinches of Tylose®, CMC or Gum Tragacanth can be kneaded to strengthen the sugarpaste until it is easier to handle. This will also make the sugarpaste dry harder.

stick support for the head

A cocktail stick or dowel can be used as a support for the head, but if an edible support is required, make sugar sticks in advance so that they are dry and hard. These can be made from strengthened sugarpaste (see above). Candy sticks are available in some sweet shops, which can also be used as a support.

glue

Sugarpaste or modelling paste should stick to itself when pressed lightly. If not, dampen (not wet) with a paintbrush over one of the surfaces before pressing gently together. Care should be taken only to make the surface damp and tacky, not wet. Some people like to use sugar glue, made by mixing a small amount of sugarpaste with water. Other glues can be made using a small pinch of Tylose®, CMC or Gum Tragacanth mixed with a few teaspoons of water, and left for a few hours to thicken.

To make a glue for parts which refuse to stick, use a small pinch of the coloured sugarpaste you are using and mash it together with a few drops of water until it forms 'gunge'- a sticky, stringy-looking paste. Royal Icing is also a useful glue for parts which refuse to stick, or fall off after the model is dry.

colours

I use strong edible paste colours for mixing into the sugarpaste. When wanting to make pale colours, mix the chosen colour until it is a stronger colour than you will need into a much smaller piece of paste; then gradually mix in small pieces of the coloured paste to the main piece until you get the shade you require. Commercially available coloured sugarpastes are a very useful time-saver - particularly for the dark colours like black and red, or if you want to make a number of the same coloured models. The colours I have used for the skin colours are various mixes and shades of Paprika, Autumn Leaf, Chestnut and Dark Brown.

modelling tools

On the next two pages I have listed some of the tools I find useful in modelling.

useful tools for modelling

(anticlockwise from bottom left)

design wheel with changeable heads - large stitch, wavy- line and straight-line
quilting tool - fine stitch
cutting wheel
drinking straw
cotton bud
cocktail stick/ toothpick
texturing tool
fine palette knife
tweezers
small rolling pin
fine pointed scissors
vegetable oil to stop paste sticking to hands/ board
fine grater and pot scourer - as texturing embossers
petal veining tool
Dresden tool
balltool/dogbone tool
zig-zag scissors

cutters/embossers

small plunger blossom and heart cutters
calyx cutter
butterfly cutter
tiny petal (broderie anglaise)
bow cutter
ribbon/ strip cutter
quilt embosser
flower cutter
oval, round and square cutters
leaf pattern embosser
small star cutter
plain piping tubes -
(different sizes for cutting tiny circles)

brushes

0000 for detail on faces
large blusher brush for dusting large areas
(e.g. satin effect on quilt for elf)
alcohol in dropper bottle for painting
dusting brush

**waterbrushes - medium for dampening
surfaces for joining;
fine for defining and cleaning painted
faces**

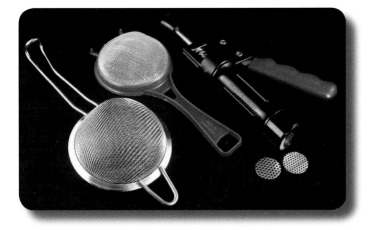

tools for fluff/fur/hair

sieve/ tea strainer
clay gun

head mould

For the babies faces in this book I use ®Holly Products Baby Head Mould. The measurements for the body parts relate to the medium size head. Other sizes and other moulds may be used, or the face can be modelled by hand. I use Sugar Mexican Paste for the face and hands. Please adapt the method for your chosen material; a cocktail stick/toothpick can be used to support the head for non-edible models, a candy stick or strengthened dried sugar stick for edible models. **Do not** put vegetable fat or cornflour into the mould as it can take away the detail in the finished face.

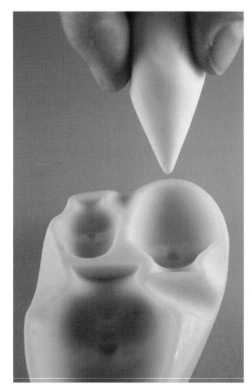

Make a ball of flesh-coloured paste slightly larger than the size of the head you want. Make sure that the ball is really smooth, as any creases may show up in the finished head. Form into a pointed cone shape. Rub a small amount of cornflour over the surface of the cone shape to dry the surface slightly. The point of the paste goes into the nose section of the mould. This will help to create the nose. If you don't start with a cone shape of paste, an air pocket can form when pushing the paste into the mould, which will make it very difficult to create the facial features.

Press down firmly into the mould using the end of a small rolling pin for extra pressure. Place dampened sugar stick on the back of the paste in the mould leaving a length of the stick at the neck end to support the head for painting, and for support when attaching the head to the body. Squash the paste together over the stick.

Remove from the mould by holding the stick. Cut off any excess paste. The back of the head will be hidden under a hat so only the rough shape is needed at this stage. The head can be worked on straight away with care, but it is easier to use if left to dry until firm. It is useful to make several heads at a time and store those for future use or for practising painting faces.

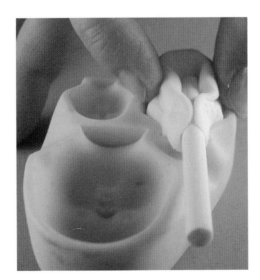

painting faces

A very fine paintbrush is needed to paint the detail, particularly for open eyes. I use a 0000 paintbrush. To avoid damaging the head while painting hold it only by the stick under the neck. This also helps when turning the head round to paint the second eye, as it can be easier to paint in one direction. When painting the eyelash line, start from side of the eye nearest the nose and paint the line outwards resulting in a finer end to the painted line.

When painting the faces I use edible powder colours mixed with alcohol. The alcohol dries quickly, which is useful when painting the open eyes. If you prefer to use water rather than alcohol, allow extra time for each layer of colour in the eyes to dry fully before painting the next colour.

Add a few drops of alcohol to your chosen powder colour on a paint palette, plate or tile. Test the strength of the colour and thickness of the line by painting onto a tissue or the back of the moulded baby head (this will be covered with a hat, so will not be seen) before painting onto the face. Make sure that each layer of colour is dry before painting another colour.

Small mistakes can be corrected and fine adjustments made using a slightly damp, clean fine paintbrush. I like to use a fine waterbrush (a paintbrush filled with water). For larger mistakes clean with a slightly damp cotton bud. In both cases leave the surface to dry before trying to paint again, or the colours might run.

sleeping baby face

This is the easiest one to start with, especially if you haven't tried painting faces before. Paint the colours pale and soft. This will look more delicate than bold colours.

lips - use a dusky pink or peach, or soft pearly pink. Paint the shape of the lips simply, keep them small, following the shape made by the mould.

eyelash line and eyebrows - use dark brown, but mixed with enough alcohol to make it appear pale. Paint a single line along the bottom line of each eye and above each eye for the eyebrows.

For this book I keep the painting simple but, if you want to paint in more detail, you could paint individual eyelashes.

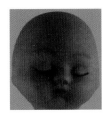

awake baby face

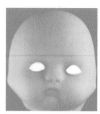

eyeball

Paint the whole eyeball with white, or pearl white. Pearl white will make the eye look shinier than plain white.

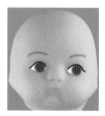

iris

Paint a large circle of your chosen colour making sure that it covers the white from top to bottom - only a small amount of the white will be seen either side of the colour. Brown, blue and green can be used in various shades. Pearly blues and greens can be used to give the eyes a shiny appearance. Paint the iris of the eyes slightly to one side to avoid getting a cross-eyed look.

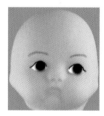

eyelash line and eyebrows

Use black or dark brown mixed with alcohol. Paint a single line along the top line of each eye, starting at the edge nearest the nose and following the top edge around the eyeball. I don't usually paint the lower lashes for the open eyes.
For the eyebrows use dark brown mixed with enough alcohol to make it appear pale. Paint a single line above each eye.

pupil

Paint a circle of black in the centre of the iris. Make sure that the black is large enough to touch the eyelash line, otherwise the eyes can look a bit staring and scary.

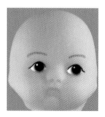

dot of light

A <u>very</u> tiny white highlight dot can be used on eyes to make the eyes look more shiny. Paint with a very fine paintbrush or the tip of a cocktail stick dipped in white mixed with alcohol (best left out if you do not have a steady hand!)

lips

Use a dusky pink or peach, or soft pearly pink. Paint the shape of the lips simply, keep them small, following the shape made by the mould.

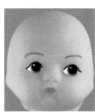

open mouth

A small triangle mouth can be made simply by pushing in the small end of a Dresden tool. Different shaped mouths can be made using a cocktail stick; or a sharp pointed knife.

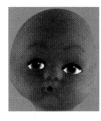

hair

Can be painted. Use brush strokes from the mould-line down over the forehead to look wispy.

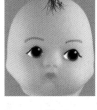

Here are some examples of finished faces

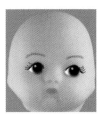

modelling baby hands

Make two 0.5cm balls of flesh-coloured Mexican paste and form into cone shapes. Flatten slightly and cut a tiny piece out with fine pointed scissors to form mitten shape and thumb.

To form the fingers indent a line with a knife or fine pointed scissors half-way across the length of the hand, then one line either side (three indents to form four fingers). When shaping small fingers, it is best **not** to cut right through, just indent and round off the top of the fingers. Curve fingers slightly inwards to form a soft fist. Make sure that you make a left and right hand. Hands can be used in the model straight away, or left to dry for later use.

Alternatively, use the hand mould (see page 22).

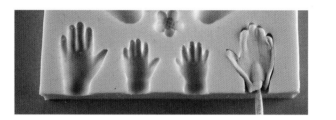

basic shapes

To make it easier for you to adapt parts for the different characters, I have used similar shapes for the body pieces of each baby.

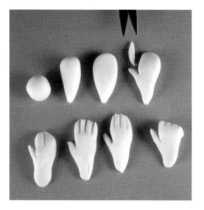

body

Make an egg shape for the body, roughly twice the size of the head using sugarpaste (or strengthened sugarpaste). The body can be made to sit up or lie down. The bottom can be marked with a nappy changing flap if wanted; indent straight lines, then use the end of a drinking straw or a tiny circle cutter to make buttons. Mark button holes with a cocktail stick.

tummy

Roll out sugarpaste thinly. Cut out using a small oval cutter. Press the surface with a textured sponge to make a fur effect, and to thin around the edge. Mark around the edge with a stitching-wheel. Use a small palette knife to release the paste from the surface. Stick onto the body.

arms

Make a 3cm ball of paste, roll into a 7cm long sausage. Indent both ends with a ball tool and dampen. Attach the hands to the arms with the thumbs facing forwards and the fingers curving down to the surface.

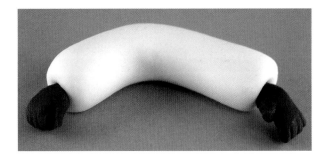

legs and feet for animal outfits

Make a ball of paste the same size as the head. Roll one end between finger and thumb to form a short leg with a fatter end for the foot. Squeeze and shape fat end to form large foot and indent two lines to form three toes using a blunt knife or Dresden tool. On the sole of the foot make shallow indents for three toe-pads and one large pad using a small balltool/dogbone tool. Make three tiny balls - one for each toe - and one slightly larger for the footpad. Stick onto sole of foot and gently press into place. Make both feet at the same time to keep the sizes the same.

fluff, fur or hair

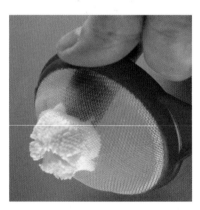

Fluff can be made using a number of different tools, each giving a slightly different effect:

•sieve or tea strainer - nylon or metal mesh

Push a small piece of sugarpaste through the mesh of a dry nylon or metal fine sieve to the other side using your thumb or the end of a small rolling pin. Different lengths of fluff can be achieved. Dampen the area on the model to be covered, then using a blunt knife remove a small amount of the fluff from the mesh. Press gently into place using a cocktail stick - do not use fingers to press it on as it may flatten the fluff.

•clay gun using fine holes; or garlic press

These are both useful for making longer strands of hair, as well as short fluff and fur. When making long hair I use Mexican paste as it is easier to separate the strands to attach in smaller clumps. Use the same method as above for sticking the hair/fluff/fur onto the body.

texturing

Surfaces can be textured using a variety of everyday materials such as scouring pad, toothbrush, fine grater, or sponge. A wire texturing brush is available along with various commercial texturing mats and embossers. Try out different methods on a spare piece of paste until you achieve the effect you want.

The lamb has been textured using a scouring pad, and the fluff made with paste squeezed through a clay gun.

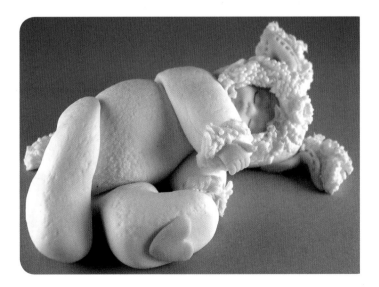

mould for small items

I have had a non-stick silicone rubber mould produced to help when making some of the small pieces for the models in the book. It can be used with Mexican paste, and other non-edible pastes. For best effect use slightly less paste than would be needed to fill each little mould. Push paste in with a Dresden tool to ensure that all the detail appears. Remove any excess paste from the mould and push the paste into the mould again. Before removing from the mould make sure you can see the edges of the mould. Remove from the mould by turning the mould over, so that the item can pop out, or help it out with the point of a cocktail stick. Care should be taken with silicone rubber moulds not to damage them; do not bend them backwards, do not use with sharp metal tools, do not store with metal cutters or tools.

 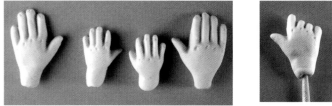

hands

Two sizes. It can be useful to push a cocktail stick into the wrist-end of the hand to help it out of the mould, and to hold the hand when adapting it's position. Hands can be adapted by cutting down between the fingers and curved to give more movement. The stick can later be removed by gently twisting and pulling it out. The hand mould has been made on the edge so that a whole arm can be modelled without a join.

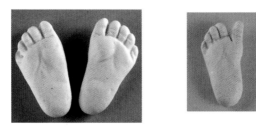

baby soles of feet

I used it for the monkey - to make it look more like a monkey foot I cut down through the toes. Could be used to make babies with bare legs.

bird wings

For the angel. Can be dusted or painted with non-toxic pearl powders. Could also be used as an alternative for baby birds and ducks.

butterfly wings

For the fairy and elf. Can be dusted or painted.

crown

Curl round to form a crown for the frog. Paint with metallic colours, or stick non-toxic glitter. Could be used as a crown or tiara for a princess.

elf ears

Tiny ears for the elf or fairy.

bow

Could be used for teddy, reindeer or penguin

bell

For the collar on the kitten and the reindeer. Could also be stuck on the end of the reindeer antlers. Could be used for the tips on the clown hat,

small star

For the angel. Could be used for the clown hat.

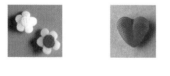

small flower and small heart

Could be used on the clown hat, or as buttons, or on the fairy.

beak

As the peaked hat for the duck. Could also be used for the penguin.

bunny

bunny

face and hands

Make your preferred choice of head and hands as shown in the introduction, paint the face and leave to dry.

body

Make an egg shape for the body, roughly twice the size of the head using sugarpaste (or strengthened sugarpaste). Sit the body up or lying down.

tummy

Roll out sugarpaste thinly. Cut out using a small oval cutter. Press the surface with a textured sponge to make a fur effect, and to thin around the edge. Mark around the edge with a stitching-wheel. Use a small palette knife to release the paste from the surface. Stick onto the body.

legs and feet

Make two balls each the same size as the head. Roll one end between finger and thumb to form a short leg with a fatter end for the foot. Squeeze and shape fat end to form large foot and indent two lines to form three toes using a blunt knife or Dresden tool. On the soles of the feet make shallow indents for three toe-pads and one large pad using a small balltool/dogbone tool. Make six tiny pale pink balls - one for each toe - and two slightly larger for the footpads. Stick onto soles of feet. Attach the legs to the body.

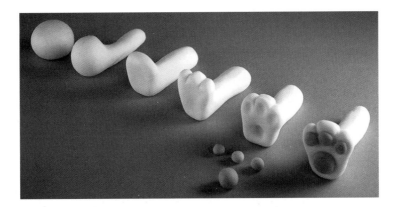

arms

Make a 3cm ball of paste, roll into a 7cm long sausage. Indent both ends with a ball tool and dampen. Attach the hands to the arms with the thumbs facing forwards and the fingers curving down to the surface. Lift the arms onto the body and position the hands where wanted using a damp brush. Make a dip for the head to sit in.

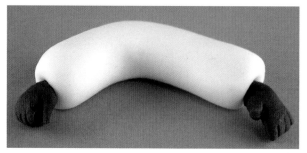

bunny head

Make a ball of sugarpaste the same size as the head. Roll out to form a large flattened circle approximately 6cm across. Dampen round the edge of the circle. Gently ease the paste to sit neatly round the face, starting halfway down the forehead, covering the back of the head. Join up under the chin, then cut off any excess paste. If using a sugar stick to support the head make a hole the same size in the top of the body first. Dampen where the head will join. Attach head by pushing the sugar stick down into the top of body, but be careful not to push too far as this will distort the figure. If making a sleeping baby, tilt the head over to one side.

ears

Make two 1cm balls of sugarpaste and form into flattened cones 3cm long. Make two 0.5cm balls in coloured sugarpaste and flatten into smaller similar shaped cones. Place the coloured cone on top of the white cone and impress the centre using a Dresden tool. Mark around the edge with a stitching-wheel. Gently squeeze the tip and the base to form an ear shape. Attach the ears side by side at the back of the head pointing straight upwards. Ears can be flopped forward for effect if required.

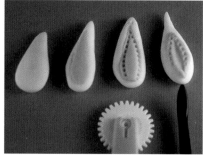

fluffy cheeks and tail

Make fluff as shown on pages 20-21 in the introduction. Dampen the body where the fluff is going to go. Make two small white fluffy cheeks. Attach to the edge of the hat overhanging the forehead. Press gently into place using a cocktail stick - do not use fingers to press it on as it may flatten the fluff. Make a fluffy tail and stick gently in position. Make a small pink triangle for nose. Stick the nose into place.

bunny eyes

Dip a cocktail stick into black paste colour and form two eyes by gently pressing the tip into the paste between the fluffy cheeks and the ears.

alternative positions

If you would like to make the bunnies lying down as shown here, adapt the shapes of the bodies using the instructions from the elf and the fairy outfits.

clown

clown

face and hands

Make your preferred choice of head and hands as shown in the introduction, paint the face and leave to dry.

body

Make two different coloured balls of sugarpaste (or strengthened sugarpaste) each roughly the same size as the head. Cut each in half. Arrange the pieces alternately and press back together. Form into an egg shape for the body. Indent lines on the bottom to look like a nappy-changing flap, then decorate with stitching-wheel. Indent two small buttons at the top of the flap using a number 2 piping nozzle.

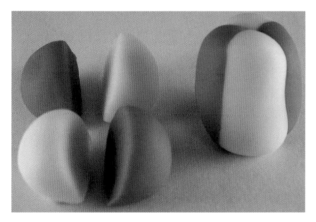

feet

Make two balls of coloured sugarpaste the same size as the head. Roll one end between finger and thumb to form a short leg. Squeeze and shape the fat end to form a boot. Press the blade of a knife across the sole to form a heel, and across the sole to look like ridges. Attach the feet to the body, dampening if necessary.

Using coloured sugarpaste, make two or three tiny balls for buttons. Attach to the front of the body and flatten. Make button holes using a No 2 piping nozzle.

arms

Roll out sugarpaste. Cut out two small circles for the frilly cuffs, and two larger circles for the ruff around the neck. Frill around the edge of each circle; different frilling tools can be used to give different textures - silk effect, lines or dots.

Make a 3cm ball of sugarpaste, roll into a 7cm long sausage. Attach the frilly cuffs to the ends. Indent both ends of the arm with a ball tool and dampen. Attach the hands to the arms with the thumbs facing forwards and the fingers curving down to the surface. Lift the arms onto the body and position the hands.

Make a dip for the head to sit in. Attach the frilled ruff to the top of the arms, to sit underneath the head.

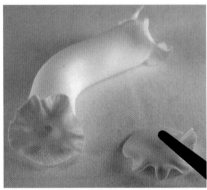

clown hat

Make two different coloured balls of sugarpaste. Form each into a short cone approximately 3cm long. Stick and smooth the fat ends together side-by-side, leaving the pointed ends apart. Hollow out the fat end by pinching with finger and thumb until it fits the back of the head. Dampen inside the hat. Gently ease the paste to sit neatly on the head and curl the pointed ends over sideways. Make a small indent in each pointed end to take a bobble. Attach head by pushing the sugar stick down into the top of body, but be careful not to push too far as this will distort the figure.

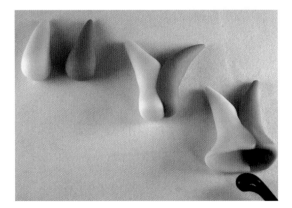

hair

Make brightly-coloured hair by pushing paste through a clay gun or garlic press. Attach around the edge of the hat in small clumps to look like a wig.

rope edge

Roll two different colours of paste to form thin sausages, each long enough to go around the hat. Turn them together, starting in the middle. Stick to the hat, joining together at the back.

bobbles

Make two tiny balls of coloured sugarpaste. Stick them on the end of the hat. Alternatively, attach tiny bells, flowers or stars to the point of the hat using a mould.

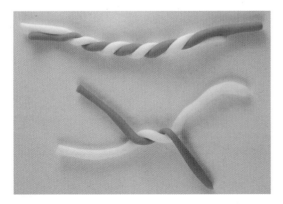

frog

frog

face and hands

Make your preferred choice of head and hands as shown in the introduction, paint the face and leave to dry.

frog head

Make a ball of green sugarpaste the same size as the head. Roll out to form a large flattened circle approximately 6cm. Dampen round the edge of the circle. Gently ease the paste to sit neatly round the face, starting halfway down the forehead. Join up under the chin, then cut off any excess paste. Using the Dresden tool, pull out the paste either side of the baby face and pinch together. Using two 1cm balls of green sugarpaste, roll out two thin sausages and stick along the both edges of the mouth to form the upper and lower lips of the frog. Pinch the corners together and tip slightly upwards to form a smile. Make two tiny holes for the nostrils. Make two indentations in the top of the head with a balltool/dogbone tool for the eyes to sit in.

arms

Make a 3cm ball of sugarpaste, roll into a 7cm long sausage. Indent both ends with a ball tool. Push the stick supporting the head through the middle of the arms. Stick the arms to the underside of the head, so that the arms look as though they are reaching up. Attach the hands to the arms.

body

Make an egg shape for the body, roughly twice the size of the head using sugarpaste (or strengthened sugarpaste). Pinch the base to form a slightly pointed bottom.

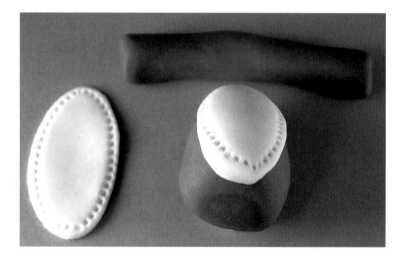

tummy

Roll out pale green sugarpaste, cut a small oval shape. Flatten slightly leaving the outside edges thinner. Decorate the outside edge with a stitching-wheel. Attach to the centre front of the body.

legs and feet

Make two balls of green sugarpaste the same size as head. Roll one end between finger and thumb to form a short leg. Squeeze and shape the fat end to form large triangular foot. Flatten the toe-end and cut out three triangles to form four toes. Indent three lines down each sole using a Dresden tool. Attach the legs to the body, dampening if necessary.

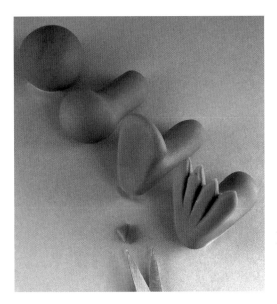

Attach head and arms to the body. If using a sugar stick to support the head make a hole the same size as the stick in the top of the body first. Dampen where the head will join. Attach head by pushing the sugar stick down into the top of body, but be careful not to push too far as this will distort the figure.

crown

Make a small crown from the mould using Mexican paste. curve it round to form a circle. Stick into position on the top of the head.

eyes

Make two 1cm balls of green sugarpaste. Make two smaller flat discs of white sugarpaste and two even smaller of black sugarpaste and attach to the front of the green balls. Stick into position on the head, each side of the crown.

piglet

piglet

face and hands

Make your preferred choice of head and hands as shown in the introduction, paint the face and leave to dry.

body

Make an egg shape for the body, roughly twice the size of the head using sugarpaste (or strengthened sugarpaste).

tummy

Roll out dark pink sugarpaste thinly. Cut out using a small oval cutter. Press the surface with a textured sponge to make a fur effect, and to thin around the edge. Mark around the edge with a stitching-wheel. Use a small palette knife to release the paste from the surface. Stick onto the body.

legs and feet

Make two pale pink sugarpaste balls the same size as head. Roll one end between finger and thumb to form a short leg. Squeeze and shape the fat end to form large foot and gently press into place, dampening if necessary. Use the mould or a heart cutter to make two dark pink hearts. Stick onto soles of feet with a dampened brush.

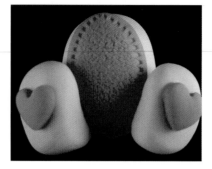

curly tail

Make a 1cm ball of pale pink Mexican paste, roll to form a long pointed cone for the tail. Coil it round cocktail stick. Stick the fat end of the tail to the body at the back.

arms

Make a 3cm ball of paste, roll into a 7cm long sausage. Indent both ends with a ball tool and dampen. Attach the hands to the arms with thumbs facing forwards and fingers curving down to the surface. Lift the arms onto the body and position the hands using a damp brush. Make a dip for the head to sit in.

piglet head

Make a ball of sugarpaste the same size as the head. Roll out to form a large flattened circle approximately 6cm. Dampen round the edge of the circle. Gently ease the paste to sit neatly round the face, starting halfway down the forehead. Join up under the chin, then cut off any excess paste. If using a sugar stick to support the head make a hole the same size in the top of the body first. Dampen where the head will join. Attach head by pushing the sugar stick down into the top of body, but be careful not to push too far as this will distort the figure.

nose

Make a 1.5cm ball of dark pink sugarpaste. Shape into an oval. Attach to head, slightly overhanging the forehead. Press in two round holes for nostrils.

ears

Using pink sugarpaste make two 1cm balls, form into 2cm cones. Make two smaller cones with dark pink paste. Indent a line down the centre of each ear, pinch to a point at the top and squeeze sides together at the base. Use stitching-wheel around the edge. Dampen and attach to the side of the head, points upwards. Pull the points of the ears down forwards.

eyes

Use a cocktail stick dipped in black paste colour to form two small black eyes above the nostrils.

teddy

teddy

The colour I use for teddy-bear brown is Autumn Leaf. For the ivory, use the same colour but much paler.

face and hands

Make your preferred choice of head and hands as shown in the introduction, paint the face and leave to dry.

body

Make an egg shape for the body, roughly twice the size of the head using sugarpaste (or strengthened sugarpaste).

tummy

Cut out a small oval from ivory paste. Press the surface with a textured sponge to make a fur effect, and to thin around the edge. Mark around the edge with a stitching-wheel. Use a small palette knife to release the paste from the surface. Stick onto the body.

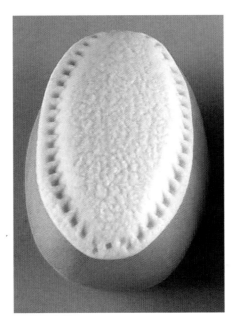

legs and feet

Make two sugarpaste balls, each the same size as the head. Roll one end between finger and thumb to form a short leg. Squeeze and shape the fat end to form a large foot. Attach the legs to the body, dampening if necessary. Make two 1cm balls of ivory sugarpaste; press with texturing sponge to form ovals smaller than the sole of the foot and attach to soles. Mark around the soles with a stitching-wheel.

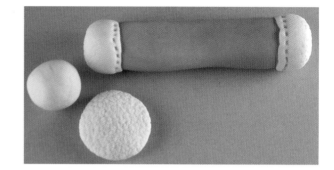

arms

Make a 3cm ball of sugarpaste, roll into a 6cm sausage. Make two 1cm balls of ivory sugarpaste, flatten slightly and texture with sponge. Attach to each end of the arms to form cuff. Mark around joining-edge with the stitching-wheel. Indent both ends with a ball tool and dampen. Attach the hands to the arms with the thumbs facing forwards and the fingers curving down to the surface. Lift the arms onto the body and position the hands using a damp brush. Make a dip for the head to sit in.

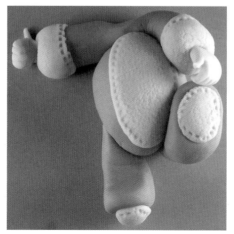

teddy head

Make a ball of sugarpaste the same size as the head. Roll out to form a large flattened circle approximately 6cm across. Dampen round the edge of the circle. Gently ease the paste to sit neatly round the face, starting halfway down the forehead. Join up under the chin, then cut off any excess paste. If using a sugar stick to support the head make a hole the same size in the top of the body first. Dampen where the head will join. Attach head by pushing the sugar stick down into the top of body, but be careful not to push too far as this will distort the figure.

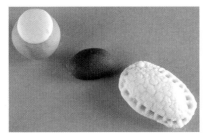

cheeks and nose

Make two small ovals of ivory sugarpaste. Texture the surface with sponge. Attach to the edge of the hat overhanging the forehead and press into place. Make a black or dark brown oval for the nose and stick it into place.

ears and eyes

Make two 0.5cm balls of sugarpaste. Make two smaller balls of ivory sugarpaste and press gently on top of the larger balls. Stick the ears in place on top of the head. Support the back of the ear with a finger and press a large dogbone tool in to cup the inside of the ear. Use a cocktail stick dipped in black paste colour to form two eyes.

Make a bow using Mexican paste. Powder or paint the whole bow with pearl colour. Stick in place.

alternative

Use different colours to create different teddies. Black and white will make a panda. Eyes for the panda are made with pieces of black and white paste

45

kitten

kitten

Although I have made my kittens in black and white, there are many other colours of kittens which could be made using the same method.

face and hands

Make your preferred choice of head and hands as shown in the introduction, paint the face and leave to dry.

body

Make an egg shape for the body, roughly twice the size of the head using black sugarpaste (or strengthened sugarpaste).

tummy

Roll out white sugarpaste thinly. Cut out using a small oval cutter. Press the surface with a textured sponge to make a fur effect, and to thin around the edge. Mark around the edge with a stitching-wheel. Use a small palette knife to release the paste from the surface. Stick onto the body.

tail

Roll a 2cm ball of black sugarpaste into a 5cm sausage. Roll a 0.5 cm ball of white sugarpaste attach to the end, and stick together, rolling to keep the sausage shape. Attach to the back of the body in the form of a curve.

legs and feet

Make two black sugarpaste balls each the same size as the head. Roll one end between finger and thumb to form a short leg. Squeeze and shape the fat end to form a large foot. Make two 1cm balls of white sugarpaste and flatten into ovals the same size as the base of the feet. Texture with sponge. Attach to the feet and mark round joining-edge with the stitching-wheel. On the sole of the foot, make shallow indents for three toe-pads and one large pad with a small balltool/dogbone tool.

Make six tiny pink balls; one for each toe - and two slightly larger balls for the pads of the feet. Stick onto soles of feet and gently press into place. Attach the legs to the body, dampening if necessary.

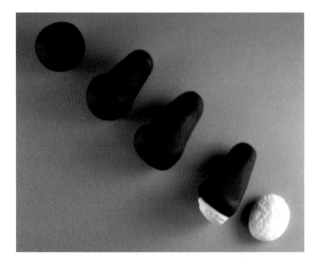

arms

Make a 3cm ball of sugarpaste, roll into a 6cm sausage. Make two 1cm balls of white sugarpaste, flatten slightly and texture with sponge. Attach to each end of the arms to form cuff. Mark round joining-edge with the stitching-wheel. Indent both ends with a ball tool and dampen. Attach the hands to the arms with the thumbs facing forwards and the fingers curving down to the surface. Lift the arms onto the body and position the hands using a damp brush. Make a dip for the head to sit in.

kitten head

Make a ball of black sugarpaste the same size as the head, roll out to form a large flattened circle approximately 6cm. Dampen round the edge of the circle. Gently ease the paste to sit neatly round the face, starting halfway down the forehead. Join up under the chin, then cut off any excess paste. If using a sugar stick to support the head make a hole the same size in the top of the body first. Dampen where the head will join. Attach head by pushing the sugar stick down into the top of body, but be careful not to push too far as this will distort the figure.

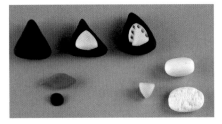

cheeks and nose

Make two small ovals of white sugarpaste. Texture the surface with sponge. Attach to the edge of the hat overhanging the forehead and press into place. Make a small pink triangle for the nose and stick it into place.

ears

Make two 1cm balls of black sugarpaste. Form into fat triangles. Make two 0.5cm balls of pink sugarpaste into triangles and place on top of the black triangles. Mark round the edge with stitching-wheel. Stick the ears in place on top of the head. Support the back of the ear with a finger and press in with a Dresden tool to cup the inside of the ear.

eyes

Make two small eye shapes of green sugarpaste and add two smaller black round centres. Attach to the head directly above the cheeks. Paint a tiny white dot on each kitten-eye to make it look shiny.

Attach a thin strip of coloured paste for a collar. Make a tiny bell shape of Mexican paste from the mould. Stick the bell onto the collar. Bell could then be painted with non-toxic gold colour.

49

puppy

puppy

face and hands

Make your preferred choice of head and hands as shown in the introduction, paint the face and leave to dry.

spots

Make a few very small irregular spots of black sugarpaste to stick onto the body parts. Keep in a plastic bag until needed.

body

Make an egg shape for the body, roughly twice the size of the head using white sugarpaste (or strengthened sugarpaste). Stick a few black spots on the body, flattening onto the surface.

tail

Make a 1cm ball of sugarpaste, roll to form a long pointed cone for the tail. Stick the fat end of the tail to the body at the back. Flick the tail up at the end.

legs and feet

Make two balls each the same size as the head. Stick two or three black blobs on each, flattening onto the surface. Roll one end between finger and thumb to form a short leg with a fatter end for the foot. Squeeze and shape fat end to form large foot and indent two lines to form three toes using a blunt knife or Dresden tool. On the sole of each foot make shallow indents for three toe-pads and one large pad using a small balltool/dogbone tool. Attach the legs to the body.

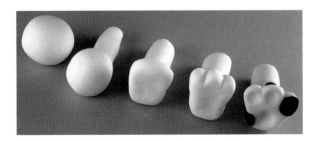

Make six tiny pale pink balls - one for each toe - and two slightly larger for the footpad. Stick onto soles of the feet and gently press into place.

arms

Make a 3cm ball of white paste, stick on two or three black blobs, flattening onto the surface. Roll into a 7cm long sausage. Indent both ends with a ball tool. Stick the arms onto the body. Make a dip for the head to sit in. Attach the hands to the arms.

head

Make a ball of white sugarpaste the same size as the head. Roll out to form a large flattened circle approximately 6cm across. Dampen round the edge of the circle. Gently ease the paste to sit neatly round the face, starting halfway down the forehead. Join up under the chin, then cut off any excess paste. Flatten two or three black blobs onto the surface of the head.

If using a sugar stick to support the head make a hole the same size in the top of the body first. Dampen where the head will join. Attach head by pushing the sugar stick down into the top of body, but be careful not to push too far as this will distort the figure.

cheeks and nose

Make two small ovals of white sugarpaste. Attach to the edge of the hat overhanging the forehead and press into place. Indent a few dots on each cheek with a cocktail stick. Make a small black triangle for nose. Stick the nose into place.

eyes

Make two tiny ovals of white sugarpaste. Make two even smaller black dots and stick in place on the white ovals. Stick the eyes onto the head.

ears

Make two 1cm balls (one black and one white) and form into flattened cones 3cm long. Mark round the edge with a stitching-wheel. Gently squeeze the tip of the ear and the base to form ear shape. Attach the ears on the back of the head pointing straight upwards. Flop the ears down

collar

Roll a thin sausage of paste long enough to go around the neck. Flatten with fingers or a rolling pin. Attach round the back of the head.

lion

lion

face and hands

Make your preferred choice of head and hands as shown in the introduction, paint the face and leave to dry.

body

Make an egg shape for the body, roughly twice the size of the head using sugarpaste (or strengthened sugarpaste). I used different shades of Autumn Leaf as the colour.

tummy

Roll out lighter-coloured sugarpaste thinly. Cut out using a small oval cutter. Press the surface with a textured sponge to make a fur effect, and to thin around the edge. Mark around the edge with a stitching-wheel. Use a small palette knife to release the paste from the surface. Stick onto the body.

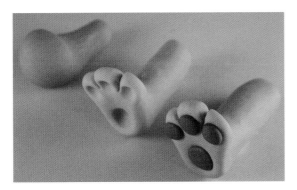

legs and feet

Make two balls each the same size as head. Roll one end between finger and thumb to form a short leg with a fatter end for the foot. Squeeze and shape the fat end to form a large foot and indent two lines to form three toes using a blunt knife or Dresden tool. On the sole of each foot make shallow indents for three toe-pads and one large pad using a small balltool/dogbone tool. Make six tiny dark brown balls - one for each toe - and two slightly larger for the footpads. Stick onto soles of feet and gently press into place. Attach the legs to the body, dampening if necessary.

arms

Make a 3cm ball of paste, roll into a 7cm long sausage. Indent both ends with a ball tool and dampen. Attach the hands to the arms with the thumbs facing forwards and the fingers curving down to the surface. Lift the arms onto the body and position the hands. Make a dip for the head to sit in.

lion head

Make a ball of sugarpaste the same size as the head. Roll out to form a large flattened circle approximately 6cm. Dampen round the edge of the circle. Gently ease the paste to sit neatly round the face, starting halfway down the forehead and neatly covering the back of the head. Join up under the chin, then cut off any excess paste. If using a sugar stick to support the head make a hole the same size in the top of the body first. Dampen where the head will join. Attach head by pushing the sugar stick down into the top of body, but be careful not to push too far as this will distort the figure.

ears

Make two 1.5cm balls of sugarpaste. Make two 0.5cm balls of lighter-coloured sugarpaste and press gently on top of the larger balls. Stick the ears in place on top of the head. Support the back of the ear with a finger and press a large balltool/dogbone tool in to cup the inside of the ear.

tail

Roll a 2cm ball of sugarpaste into a 5cm sausage. Attach underneath the body at the back in the form of a curve.

fluff

Make fluff as shown on pages 20-21 in the introduction. Dampen the body where the fluff is going to go. Form a cuff around the end of each arm, around the edge of the face, and a small piece for the tip of the tail. Press gently into place using a cocktail stick - do not use fingers to press it on as it may flatten the fluff.

lamb

lamb

Texture each body part with a textured sponge/ scourer/ grater to look like fleece before attaching to each other.

face and hands
Make your preferred choice of head and hands as shown in the introduction, paint the face and leave to dry.

body
Make an egg shape for the body, roughly twice the size of the head using sugarpaste (or strengthened sugarpaste).

lamb head
Make a ball of sugarpaste the same size as the head. Roll out to form a large flattened circle approximately 6cm across. Dampen round the edge of the circle. Gently ease the paste to sit neatly round the face, starting halfway down the forehead. Join up under the chin, then cut off any excess paste. If using a sugar stick to support the head make a hole the same size in the top of the body first. Dampen where the head will join. Attach head by pushing the sugar stick down into the top of body, but be careful not to push too far as this will distort the figure.

arms

Make a 3cm ball of paste, roll into a 7cm long sausage. Texture in the same way as the body. Indent both ends with a ball tool. Wrap the arms around from the back of the neck, making sure that the top arm hides the front of the neck. Attach the hands to the arms.

legs and feet

Make two sugarpaste balls, each the same size as the head. Roll one end between finger and thumb to form a short leg. Squeeze and shape the fat end to form a large foot. Attach the legs to the body, dampening if necessary. Texture in the same way as the body. Use the heart mould or a heart cutter to make two small hearts of peach paste. Stick onto the soles of the feet.

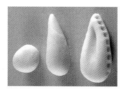

ears

Using peach sugarpaste make two 1cm balls, form into 2cm cones. Indent a line down the centre of each ear, pinch to a point at the top and squeeze sides together at the base. Dampen and attach broad end to the side of head, points upwards. Pull the points of the ears down sideways at right angles.

fluff

Make fluff as shown on pages 20-21 in the introduction. Dampen the body where the fluff is going to go. Form a cuff around the end of each arm; around the edge of the face; over each ear; and a small piece for the tail. Press gently into place using a cocktail stick - do not use fingers to press it on as it may flatten the fluff.

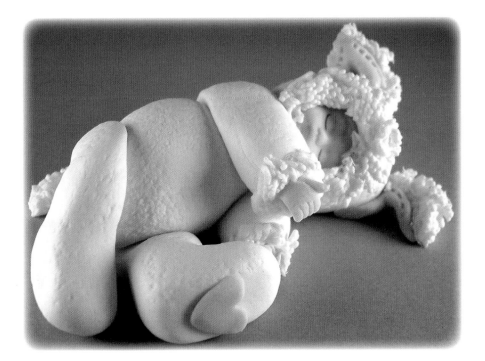

duckling

duckling

face and hands

Make your preferred choice of head and hands as shown in the introduction, paint the face and leave to dry.

body

Make an egg shape for the body, roughly twice the size of the head using sugarpaste (or strengthened sugarpaste). Pinch out a small tail at the bottom. Indent lines on the tail with a knife or cutting-wheel to look like feathers.

tummy

Roll out white sugarpaste thinly. Cut out using a small oval cutter. Press the surface with a textured sponge to make a fur effect, and to thin around the edge. Mark around the edge with a stitching-wheel. Use a small palette knife to release the paste from the surface. Stick onto the body.

legs and feet

Make two balls of red or orange paste, the same size as head and roll one end between finger and thumb to form a short leg. Squeeze and shape the fat end to form large triangular foot. Flatten the toe end and cut out two triangles to form three toes. Indent two lines down the sole using a Dresden tool. Attach the legs to the body.

arms and wings

Make a 3cm ball of yellow paste, roll into a 7cm sausage. Indent both ends with a ball tool and dampen. Press down and away with a small rolling pin to form two wing shapes, keeping a thick enough ridge for the arms. Use a cutting wheel or blunt knife to cut diagonal lines across both wings to form simple feathers. Release from the board with a small palette knife. Attach the hands to the arms with the thumbs facing forwards away from the wings and the fingers curving down to the surface. Lift the arms onto the body and position the hands over the toes. The wing feathers can be flicked-up. Make a dip for the head to sit in.

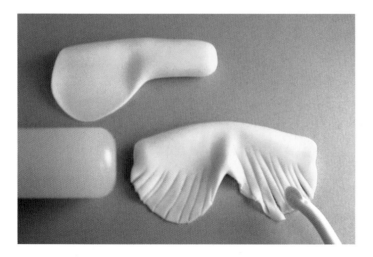

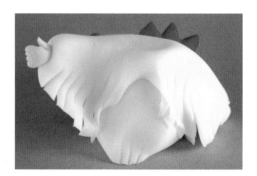

duck head

Make a ball of yellow sugarpaste the same size as the head, roll out to form a large flattened circle approx. 6cm. Dampen round the edge of the circle. Gently ease the paste to sit neatly round the face, starting halfway down the forehead. Join up under the chin, then cut off any excess paste. If using a sugar stick to support the head make a hole the same size in the top of the body first. Attach head by pushing the sugar stick down into the top of body, but be careful not to push too far as this will distort the figure. Using fine scissors, make a series of small cuts down the back of the head to form a crest.

beak

Make a 0.5cm ball of red or orange sugarpaste, roll to a 1cm sausage. Curve this over a dowel or finger and flatten the side edges. Remove from the dowel and flick up the beak tip. Attach to the hat on the forehead. Alternatively make the beak using the mould.

duck eyes

Dip a cocktail stick into black paste colour and form two eyes above the beak by gently pressing the tip into the paste.

alternatives

Using different coloured pastes you can make different ducks and birds. Here's a Mallard duck using green, purple and orange.

monkey

monkey

face and hands

Make your preferred choice of head and hands as shown in the introduction, paint the face and leave to dry.

body

Make an egg shape for the body, roughly twice the size of the head using brown sugarpaste (or strengthened sugarpaste).

tummy

Roll out lighter-coloured sugarpaste thinly. Cut out using a small oval cutter. Press the surface with a textured sponge to make a fur effect, and to thin around the edge. Mark around the edge with a stitching-wheel. Use a small palette knife to release the paste from the surface. Stick onto the body.

legs and feet

Shape two very small balls of lighter-coloured sugarpaste into monkey feet; make a pair of baby feet from the mould, cut down between the large toe and the other toes, gently squeeze the sides of the sole together to make the foot narrower. Make two brown sugarpaste balls, each slightly smaller than the head. Roll one end between finger and thumb to form a short leg. Squeeze and shape the fat end to form a large foot. Stick the monkey feet onto the base of each leg. Attach the legs to the body, curving them round so that the feet are facing each other.

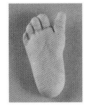

monkey head

Make a ball of brown sugarpaste the same size as the head. Roll out to form a large flattened circle approximately 6cm. Dampen round the edge of the circle. Gently ease the paste to sit neatly round the face, starting with half-way down the forehead. Join up under the chin, then cut off any excess paste.

arms

Make a 3cm ball of brown sugarpaste, roll into a 7cm long sausage. Indent both ends with a ball tool. Push the stick supporting the head through the middle of the arms. Stick the arms to the underside of the head, so that the arms look as though they are reaching up. Attach the hands to the arms.

If using a sugar stick to support the head make a hole the same size in the top of the body first. Dampen where the head will join. Attach head by pushing the sugar stick down into the top of body, but be careful not to push too far as this will distort the figure.

eyes

Cut out a small heart shape with lighter-coloured sugarpaste. Cut off the pointed end. Make two tiny ovals of white sugarpaste. Make two even smaller black dots and stick in place on the white ovals. Stick the eyes onto the head.

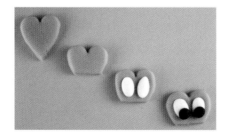

ears

Make two 1cm balls of brown sugarpaste and place a smaller lighter-coloured ball on the front of each and press gently. Stick the ears in place on the sides of the head, support the back of the ear with a finger and press a small dogbone tool in to cup the inside of the ear.

Make a long thin sausage of lighter-coloured sugarpaste. Stick it around the edge of the face and around the heart-shape.

Make a small tuft of hair using sugarpaste pushed through a garlic press or clay gun. Stick on top of the head.

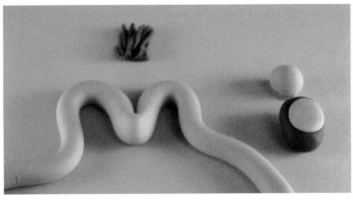

tail

Roll a long thin curled-up tail from brown sugarpaste. Attach to the bottom.

bumble bee

bumble bee

face and hands

Make your preferred choice of head and hands as shown in the introduction, paint the face and leave to dry.

body

Make an egg shape for the body, roughly twice the size of the head using black sugarpaste (or strengthened sugarpaste). Pinch the base to form a sting on the bottom.

tummy

Roll out yellow sugarpaste. Cut out a small oval shape. Also roll out black sugarpaste. Cut the black sugarpaste into 0.5cm wide strips using a strip-cutter or knife. Stick the strips across the yellow oval to give the appearance of stripes. Cut the striped tummy with an oval cutter to neaten the edge. Press with textured sponge. Mark the edges of the strips and the edge of the oval with a stitching-wheel. Attach the striped oval to the centre front of the body, dampening if necessary.

wings

Roll out white sugarpaste or strengthened sugarpaste, cut a 3.5cm circle and cut in half.

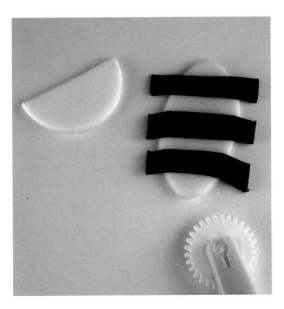

legs and feet

Make two black sugarpaste balls, each the same size as the head. Roll one end between finger and thumb to form a short leg. Squeeze and shape the fat end to form a large foot. Attach the legs to the body, dampening if necessary. Make two 1cm balls of yellow sugarpaste, flatten to form the same shape and size as the sole of the foot and attach to soles of the feet.

arms

Make a 3cm ball of black sugarpaste, roll into a 7cm sausage. Indent both ends with a ball tool and dampen. Attach the hands to the arms. Attach the white half-circles to the back of the arm as wings. Lift the arms onto the body and position the hands and wings. Make a dip for the head to sit in.

bee head

Make a ball of black sugarpaste the same size as the head, roll out to form a large flattened circle approximately 6cm. Dampen round the edge of the circle. Gently ease the paste to sit neatly round the face, starting halfway down the forehead. Join up under the chin, then cut off any excess paste. If using a sugar stick to support the head make a hole the same size in the top of the body first. Dampen where the head will join. Attach head by pushing the sugar stick down into the top of body, but be careful not to push too far as this will distort the figure.

eyes and antennae

Make two 1cm balls of black sugarpaste for eyes, form into ovals and press onto the surface of a sieve or similar to give the surface a patterned texture. Attach to the head. Paint or dust over the raised surface of the bee-eyes with a pearl or metallic colour.

Make two tiny balls of black sugarpaste and form into two pointed cones for antennae. Attach to the top of the head.

fluff

Make fluff as shown on pages 20-21 in the introduction. Dampen the body where the fluff is going to go. Attach yellow fluff on the soles and around the ends of the arms to look like pollen; also around the face bringing it to a point on the forehead.

fairy

fairy

wings

Make butterfly wings from Mexican paste. Use edible pearl colours to dust or paint the surface. Leave to dry.

face and hands

Make your preferred choice of head and hands as shown in the introduction, paint the face and leave to dry.

lying-down body with arms outstretched

Use paste approximately three times the size of the head. Form into a long pointed oval. Cut down into the narrow end. Turn the cut edges towards the surface, which will leave the smooth curved surface upwards. Indent the ends of the arms where the hands will go.

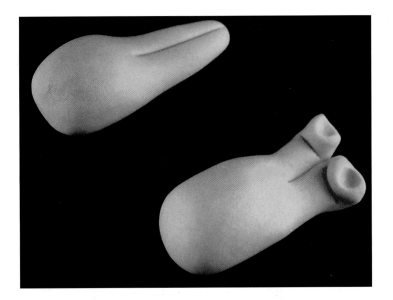

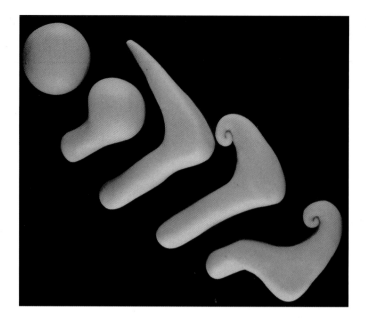

legs and feet

Make two sugarpaste balls, each slightly smaller than the head. Roll one end between finger and thumb to form a short leg. Squeeze and shape the fat end to form a pixie boot with pointed toe. Attach the legs to the body, knees bent, feet in the air.

blossoms

Roll out Mexican paste thinly. Cut out little flowers using the tiny blossom cutter set. Stick straight onto the body and ends of arms using the plunger to push the blossom into place.

Stick the hands in position.

fairy head

Cut the support-stick slightly longer than the neck. Attach head by pushing the stick down into the top of arms, looking forward. Make hair using a clay gun or garlic press. As the hair is part of the fancy-dress outfit it can be thick and brightly-coloured. Attach small clumps of hair to the head to gradually build up the shape of the wig.

Make a slight indentation on the back to help support the wings. Stick the wings in position. You might need to use a sugar glue, or a 'gunge' to make it stay in place (a small amount of paste mixed to a sticky paste with a little water).

Make a hat with petals cut out of different shaped petal cutters and different coloured sugarpaste or Mexican paste. For a softer effect the petals could also be powdered with edible food colours. Thin the edges of the petals - I use a textured petal veiner tool. Stick the hat onto the wig, making a small dip in the middle as you push it on. Make a tiny green stem, thinning to a point at the end. Stick the fat end into the middle of the flower, and curl the thin end.

optional extra - fairy ears
Make a pair of fairy ears from the mould. Dampen the head where the ears will go and stick them onto the head.

elf

elf

wings

Make butterfly wings from Mexican paste. Use edible pearl colours to dust or paint the surface. Leave to dry.

face and hands

Make your preferred choice of head and hands as shown in the introduction, paint the face and leave to dry.

quilt

Roll out sugarpaste thickly. Emboss the surface with the Patchwork Cutters® Quilt Embosser. Cut the paste to the size of the embosser. Brush the whole surface of the quilt with a pearl powder colour. I use a large blusher brush for dusting large areas. Alternatively it can look very effective to dust the squares of the quilt with different colours with a smaller dusting brush. Smooth over the cut edges with your finger. Gather the edges of the quilt under towards one end to give the baby something to cuddle and rest it's head on.

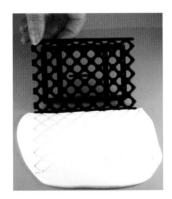

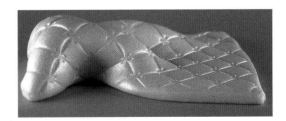

elf hat

Make a 2cm ball of green sugarpaste, form a pointed cone approximately 4cm long. Hollow out the fat end by pinching with finger and thumb until it fits the back of the head. Dampen inside the hat. Gently ease the paste to sit neatly round the face and point the end upwards, curling the tip.

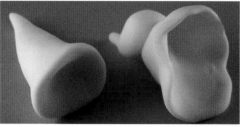

body

Make an egg shape for the body, roughly twice the size of the head using sugarpaste (or strengthened sugarpaste). Mark the shape of a nappy-changing flap on the bottom. Use tiny leaf embossers/cutters to make a leafy pattern on the body. Attach head by pushing the sugar stick down into the top of body, but be careful not to push too far as this will distort the figure.

arms

Make a 3cm ball of green sugarpaste, roll into a 7cm sausage. Indent both ends with a ball tool. Emboss with the same pattern as on the body. Stick the arms onto the body to make it look like the baby is cuddling the quilt. Attach the hands to the arms with the thumbs facing forwards. Make an indentation to hold the wings. Stick the wings in place.

legs and feet

Make two green sugarpaste balls, each slightly smaller than the head. Roll one end between finger and thumb to form a short leg. Squeeze and shape the fat end to form a pixie boot with pointed toe. Emboss with the same pattern as on the body. Attach the legs to the body, dampening if necessary.

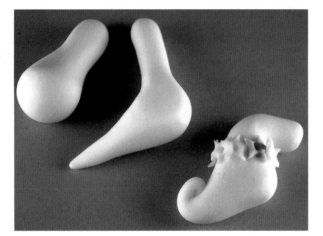

Roll out two or three colours of sugarpaste. Cut out tiny stars and stick them around the edge of the hat, sleeves and ankles.

elf ears

Using the mould make two ears of flesh-coloured Mexican paste to match the baby's face (as this is an outfit it does not have to be a perfect match). Dampen the head where the ears will go and stick them in position.

bat

bat

face and hands

Make your preferred choice of head and hands as shown in the introduction. I made the hands for the bat in coloured paste to look like gloves. Paint the face and leave to dry.

body

Make an egg shape for the body, roughly twice the size of the head using black sugarpaste (or strengthened sugarpaste).

tummy

Cut a small oval from rolled-out purple sugarpaste. Press it with textured sponge, then decorate the outside edge with a stitching-wheel. Attach to the centre front of the body, dampening if necessary.

legs and feet

Make two black sugarpaste balls, each slightly smaller than the head. Roll one end between finger and thumb to form a short leg. Squeeze and shape the fat end to form a foot. Attach the legs to the body, dampening if necessary. Make six 1cm thin strands of purple sugarpaste. Stick three on each foot, joining together at the heel.

wings and arms

Roll out purple sugarpaste or strengthened sugarpaste. Cut out two bat wings; cut a 3.5cm circle in half, cut four little curves using a smaller round cutter around the curved edge. Mark three indentations on the surface of the wings with a Dresden tool.

Make a 3cm ball of black sugarpaste, roll into a 7cm sausage. Indent both ends with a ball tool and dampen. Attach the hands to the arms with the thumbs facing forwards and the fingers curving down to the surface. Lift the arms onto the body and position the hands. Stick the wings in place along the back of each arm. Flatten the top centre of the arms gently with your finger to make a dip for the head to sit in.

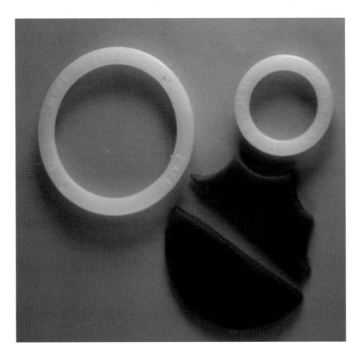

bat head

Make a ball of black sugarpaste the same size as the head, roll out to form a large flattened circle approximately 6cm. Pinch the edge to form one point for the forehead. Dampen round the edge. Gently ease the paste to sit neatly round the face, starting with the point halfway down the forehead. Join up under the chin, then cut off any excess paste. If using a sugar stick to support the head make a hole the same size in the top of the body first. Dampen where the head will join. Attach head by pushing the sugar stick down into the top of body, but be careful not to push too far as this will distort the figure.

bat face

Make a long thin sausage of purple sugarpaste. Stick it to the edge of the hat around the face bringing it to a point on the forehead.

ears

Make two 1cm balls of black sugarpaste. Form into fat triangles. Make two 0.5cm balls of purple sugarpaste into triangles and place on top of the black triangles. Mark a groove down inside each ear with a Dresden tool. Mark round the edge with stitching-wheel. Stick the ears in place on the side of the head. Tweak the tips of the ears.

pumpkin

pumpkin

face and hands

Make your preferred choice of head and hands as shown in the introduction, paint the face and leave to dry.

body

Make an ball shape for the body, roughly three times the size of the head using orange sugarpaste (or strengthened sugarpaste). Mark vertical lines to look like a pumpkin. Roll out black sugarpaste. Cut three small triangles and stick them to the pumpkin to make two eyes and a nose. Also cut out a mouth shape and stick it on.

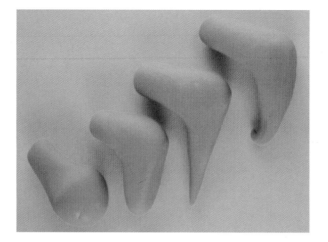

legs and feet

Make two green sugarpaste balls, each slightly smaller than the head. Roll one end between finger and thumb to form a short leg. Squeeze and shape the fat end to form a pixie boot with pointed toe. Attach the legs to the body, dampening if necessary.

arms

Make a 3cm ball of green sugarpaste, roll into a 7cm sausage. Indent both ends with a ball tool. Attach the hands to the arms with the thumbs facing forwards and the fingers curving down to the surface. Lift the arms onto the body dampening if necessary. Position the hands. Flatten the top centre of the arms gently with your finger to make a dip for the head to sit in.

head

Make a ball of orange sugarpaste the same size as the head. Roll out to form a large flattened circle approximately 6cm. Dampen round the edge of the circle. Gently ease the paste to sit neatly round the face, starting half-way down the forehead. Join up under the chin, then cut off any excess paste. Mark vertical lines to look like a pumpkin. If using a sugar stick to support the head make a hole the same size in the top of the body first. Dampen where the head will join. Attach head by pushing the sugar stick down into the top of body, but be careful not to push too far as this will distort the figure.

Roll out green paste and cut out a green flower calyx. Stick it on the top of the head. Make a tiny ball of green sugarpaste, roll to form a long pointed cone. Coil it round a cocktail stick. Stick the fat end of the coil to the middle of the calyx on the head.

little horror

little horror

face and hands

Make your preferred choice of head and hands as shown in the introduction. I made the hands with coloured paste to look like gloves. Paint the face and leave to dry.

body

Make an egg shape for the body, roughly twice the size of the head using red sugarpaste (or strengthened sugarpaste).

tummy

Roll out red sugarpaste. Also roll out black sugarpaste. Cut the black sugarpaste into 0.5cm wide strips using a strip-cutter or knife. Stick the strips across the red paste to give the appearance of stripes. Press with textured sponge. Cut the striped tummy with an oval cutter to neaten the edge. Mark the edges of the strips and the edge of the oval with a stitching-wheel. Attach the striped oval to the centre front of the body, dampening if necessary.

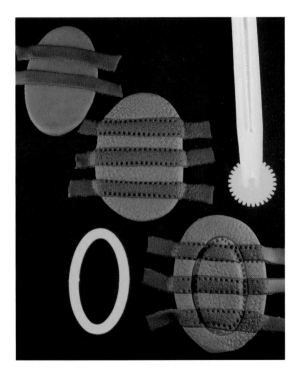

legs and feet

Make two red sugarpaste balls, each slightly smaller than the head. Roll one end between finger and thumb to form a short leg. Squeeze and shape the fat end to form a pixie boot with pointed toe. Attach the legs to the body, dampening if necessary.

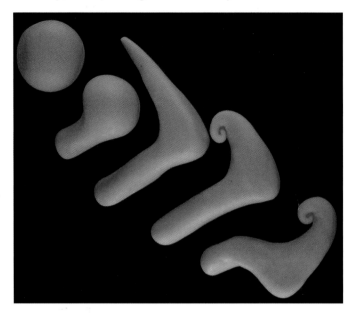

arms and wings

Roll out black sugarpaste, or strengthened sugarpaste cut out a 3.5cm circle then cut it in half with a zig-zag line.

Make a 3cm ball of red sugarpaste, roll into a 6cm sausage. Make two 1cm balls of black sugarpaste, flatten slightly and texture with sponge. Attach to each end of the arms to form cuff. Indent both ends with a balltool/dogbone tool. Attach the hands to the arms with the thumbs facing forwards and the fingers curving down to the surface. Lift the arms onto the body and position the hands. Make a dip for the head to sit in. Attach the wings to the back of the arms.

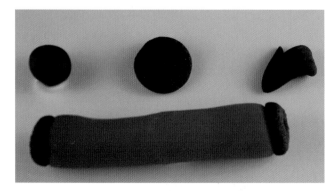

tail

Roll a long thin tail from red sugarpaste or strengthened sugarpaste. Attach to the bottom. Drape the end of the tail over the arm. Form a pointed triangle from black sugarpaste and stick it onto the end of the tail.

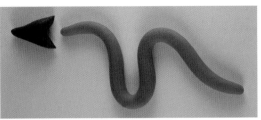

head

Make a ball of red paste the same size as the head. Roll out to form a large flattened circle approximately 6cm. Pinch edge to form one point for the forehead. Dampen round the edge of the circle. Gently ease the paste to sit neatly round the face, starting with the point half-way down the forehead. Join up under the chin, then cut off any excess paste.

If using a sugar stick to support the head make a hole the same size in the top of the body first. Dampen where the head will join. Attach head by pushing the sugar stick down into the top of body, but be careful not to push too far as this will distort the figure.

Make a long thin sausage of black sugarpaste. Stick it to the edge of the hat around the face bringing it to a point on the forehead.

horns

Using black sugarpaste make two tiny cones for the horns and attach to the top of the head, curving them to shape.

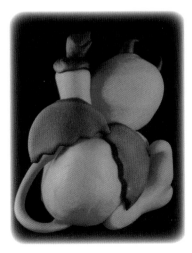

little angel

little angel

wings

Make a small pair of bird wings from Mexican paste in the mould. Take out of the mould, dust or paint with pearl white powder. Leave to dry, turning over occasionally to dry on both sides.

stars

Make a few tiny stars from Mexican paste. Dust or paint with metallic or pearl powder. If a more glittery effect is required, stick non-toxic glitter onto dry stars using edible glue. Leave to dry.

face and hands

Make your preferred choice of head and hands as shown in the introduction, paint the face and leave to dry.

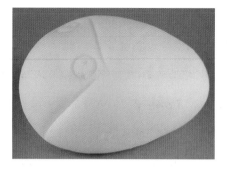

body

Make an egg shape for the body, roughly twice the size of the head using white sugarpaste (or strengthened sugarpaste). Mark the shape of a nappy-changing flap on the bottom.

legs and feet

Make two sugarpaste balls, each the same size as the head. Roll one end between finger and thumb to form a short leg. Squeeze and shape the fat end to form a large foot. Bend to form a knee. Attach the legs to the body, dampening if necessary.

head

Make a ball of sugarpaste the same size as the head. Roll out to form a large flattened circle approximately 6cm across. Dampen round the edge of the circle. Gently ease the paste to sit neatly round the face, starting halfway down the forehead. Join up under the chin, then cut off any excess paste. If using a sugar stick to support the head make a hole the same size in the top of the body first. Dampen where the head will join. Attach head by pushing the sugar stick down into the top of body, but be careful not to push too far as this will distort the figure.

arms

Make a 3cm ball of paste, roll into a 7cm long sausage. Indent both ends with a ball tool. Attach the hands to the arms with the thumbs facing forwards and the fingers curving down to the surface. Lift the arms onto the body and attach the hands.

If a satin effect is wanted, brush the surface of the paste with an edible pearl white powder mixed with alcohol. Allow the surface to dry before attaching the fluff.

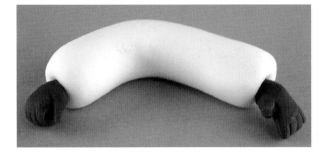

fluff

Make fluff as shown on pages 20-21 in the introduction. Dampen the body where the fluff is going to go. Make fluff to stick around the edge of the face, form a cuff around the end of each arm, and pads on each foot. Press gently into place using a cocktail stick - do not use fingers to press it on as it may flatten the fluff.

Stick the wings in place.

Stick stars in position on top of the head.

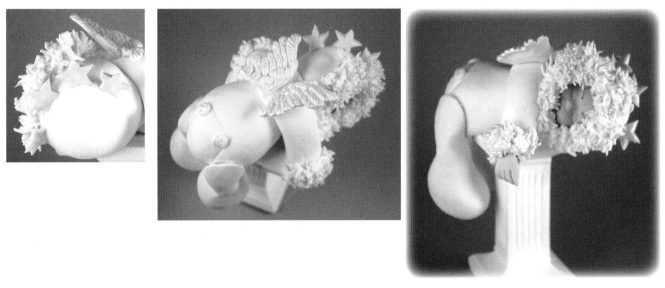

penguin

penguin

face and hands

Make your preferred choice of head and hands as shown in the introduction, paint the face and leave to dry.

body

Make an egg shape for the body, roughly twice the size of the head using white sugarpaste (or strengthened sugarpaste).

legs and feet

Make two balls of yellow or orange sugarpaste approximately the same size as head. Roll one end between finger and thumb to form a short leg. Squeeze and shape the fat end to form large triangular foot. Flatten the toe end and cut out two triangles to form three toes. Indent two lines down each sole using a Dresden tool. Attach the legs to the body.

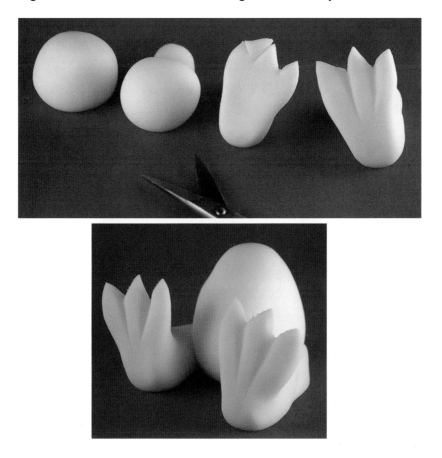

arms

Make a 3cm ball of black paste, roll into a 7cm sausage. Indent both ends with a ball tool and dampen. Attach the hands to the arms with the thumbs facing forwards and the fingers curving down to the surface. Lift the arms onto the body and position the hands. Make a dip for the head to sit in.

penguin head

Make a ball of white sugarpaste the same size as the head, roll out to form a large flattened circle approx. 6cm across. Dampen round the edge of the circle. Gently ease the paste to sit neatly round the face, starting halfway down the forehead. Join up under the chin, then cut off any excess paste. If using a sugar stick to support the head make a hole the same size in the top of the body first. Dampen where the head will join. Attach head by pushing the sugar stick down into the top of body, but be careful not to push too far as this will distort the figure.

cape

Roll out black sugarpaste, about 2mm thick. Cut out a 6cm square. Gently stretch each corner to form a point. Attach to the head with the one point forming a peak over the forehead; one forming a small tail; and the other points over the arms to give the appearance of small wings. If the paste is thick enough, the points can be stretched further.

beak

Form a 0.5cm ball of yellow sugarpaste into a small cone and attach to the edge of the hat above the forehead.

eyes

Make two tiny balls of black paste and stick them on to make the face of the penguin. Another way of making tiny perfect round shapes for the eyes is to roll out the black paste, leave the surface to dry for a few minutes, turn the paste over, and cut out using a number 2 or 3 plain piping tube/nozzle as the cutter.

alternative

For the penguin chick I used purple and white paste and stuck white 'fluff' around the face.

reindeer

reindeer

face and hands

Make your preferred choice of head and hands as shown in the introduction, paint the face and leave to dry.

antlers

Make in advance and leave to dry; make two 1cm balls of dark brown Mexican or strengthened sugarpaste. Roll to a sharp point at each end and lengthen to 5cm. Using sharp scissors, cut 1cm down into each end from the point. Make a crease slightly off centre, fold ends towards each other. Roll the folded end between your fingers to form single stem. When you have made both antlers, leave to dry in opposite positions.

body

Make an egg shape for the body, roughly twice the size of the head using brown sugarpaste (or strengthened sugarpaste).

tummy

Cut out a small oval shape of white paste. Press it with textured sponge, then decorate the outside edge with a stitching-wheel. Attach to the centre front of the body, dampening if necessary.

legs and feet

Make two sugarpaste balls, each the same size as the head. Roll one end between finger and thumb to form a short leg. Squeeze and shape the fat end to form a large foot. Attach the legs to the body, dampening if necessary. Use the heart mould or a heart cutter to make two hearts from dark brown paste. Stick onto soles of feet with a dampened brush.

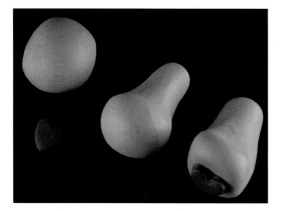 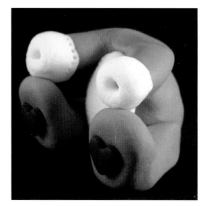

arms

Make a 3cm ball of brown sugarpaste, roll into a 6cm sausage. Make two 1cm balls of white sugarpaste, flatten slightly and texture with sponge. Attach to each end of the arms to form cuff. Mark round joining-edge with the stitching-wheel tool. Indent both ends with a balltool/dogbone tool. Attach the hands to the arms with the thumbs facing forwards and the fingers curving down to the surface. Lift the arms onto the body and position the hands. Make a dip for the head to sit in.

reindeer head

Make a ball of brown sugarpaste the same size as the head. Roll out to form a large flattened circle approximately 6cm. Dampen round the edge of the circle. Gently ease the paste to sit neatly round the face, starting halfway down the forehead. Join up under the chin, then cut off any excess paste. With a small dogbone/balltool make an indent on the edge of the hat where the nose will go; two small indents on the top of the head where the eyes will go; two small indents where the antlers will go; and two indents where the ears will go.

If using a sugar stick to support the head, make a hole the same size in the top of the body first. Dampen where the head will join. Attach head by pushing the sugar stick down into the top of body, but be careful not to push too far as this will distort the figure.

nose, eyes and ears

Stick on a small ball of red paste for the nose. Make two tiny ovals of white sugarpaste. Make two even smaller black dots and stick in place on the white ovals. Stick the eyes onto the head. Make two 0.5cm balls of sugarpaste and place a tiny pink ball on the front of each and press gently. Stick the ears in place behind the space for the antlers; support the back of the ear with a finger and press a small dogbone tool in to cup the inside of the ear.

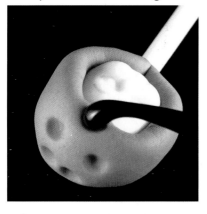

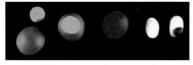

antlers

Stick the antlers in position.

tail

Make fluff as shown on pages 20-21 in the introduction. Dampen the body where the fluff is going to go. Make a white fluffy tail and stick it on.

collar and bell

Attach a thin strip of coloured paste for a collar. Make a tiny bell shape of Mexican paste from the mould. Stick the bell onto the collar. Bell can then be painted with non-toxic gold colour.

santa baby

santa baby

face and hands

Make your preferred choice of head and hands as shown in the introduction, paint the face and leave to dry.

body

Make an egg shape for the body, roughly twice the size of the head using red sugarpaste (or strengthened sugarpaste). Indent lines on the bottom to look like a nappy-changing flap. Indent two small buttons.

feet

Make two balls of black sugarpaste the same size as head. Roll one end between finger and thumb to form a short leg. Squeeze and shape the fat end to form a boot. Press the blade of a knife across the sole to form a heel, and across the sole to look like ridges. Attach the feet to the body, dampening if necessary.

waistband

Roll out white sugarpaste and cut a 1cm wide strip long enough to go round the body. Press with texturing sponge to look like fur. Mark along the edges with a stitching-wheel. Dampen the smooth side and attach round the body avoiding the changing flap. Make the join at the side of the body by sticking the two ends facing each other and cutting across with scissors.

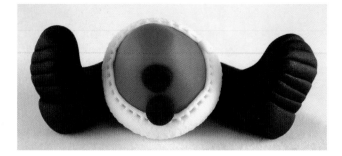

Using black sugarpaste, make two or three tiny balls for buttons. Attach to the front of the body and flatten. Make button holes using a number 2 piping nozzle.

arms

Make a 3cm ball of sugarpaste, roll into a 7cm long sausage. Make a white fur strip as before. Stick the fur around each end of the arm to form cuffs. Indent both ends of the arm with a ball tool and dampen. Attach the hands to the arms with the thumbs facing forwards and the fingers curving down to the surface. Lift the arms onto the body and position the hands. Make a dip for the head to sit in.

santa hat

Make a 2cm ball of red sugarpaste, form a short cone approximately 3cm long. Hollow out the fat end by pinching with finger and thumb until it fits the back of the head. Dampen inside the hat. Gently ease the paste to sit neatly round the face and point the end upwards. Make a small indent in the pointed end to hold the bobble. Attach head by pushing the sugar stick down into the top of body, but be careful not to push too far as this will distort the figure.

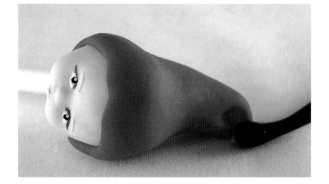

scarf

Make a 15cm long strip of white fur in the same way as before. Dampen the smooth side. Attach the strip around the face starting with one end hanging forward and the other end back over the shoulder. Cut to the length required. Make lots of small snips with fine scissors to make fringes on the ends of the scarf.

bobble

Make a fluffy ball; either by making a ball of paste and texturing it with the sponge as before; or make fluff as described in the introduction, pages 20-21. Stick onto the end of the hat.

contacts

frances mcnaughton

sugar artist and tutor

supplier of the equipment used in this book

website www.franklysweet.co.uk

email fran.mac@btinternet.com

tel 0044 (0)1892 518241

holly products

website www.hollyproducts.co.uk

tel 0044 (0)1630 655759

fpc sugarcraft moulds

website www.fpcsc.co.uk

0044 (0)117 985 3249

artista uk

modelling paste

tel 0044 1775 722844

coronet

porcelain paste

website www.coronetporcelainpaste.co.uk

tel 0044 (0)1474 705180

search press ltd

craft book publisher

website www.searchpress.com

tel 0044 (0)1892 510850

guy paul

sugarcraft and bakery supplies to the trade

website www.guypaul.co.uk

tel 0044 (0)1494 432121

design-a-cake

sugarcraft and cake decoration retail warehouse

and online shop

website www.design-a-cake.co.uk

tel 0044 (0)191 417 9697

british sugarcraft guild

website www.bsguk.org

tel 0044 (0)208 859 6943

national sugarart association

sheila lampkin

0044 (0)208 777 4445

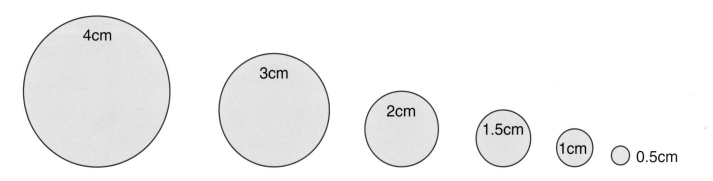